Contents

Uno

un perro

Hay un perro.

There is one dog.

Hay un suéter.

There is one jumper.

Dos

un gato

Hay dos gatos.

There are two cats.

un zapato

Hay dos zapatos.

There are two shoes.

Tres

una chica

Hay tres chicas.

There are three girls.

una silla

Hay tres sillas.

There are three chairs.

Cuatro

un pájaro

Hay cuatro pájaros.

There are four birds.

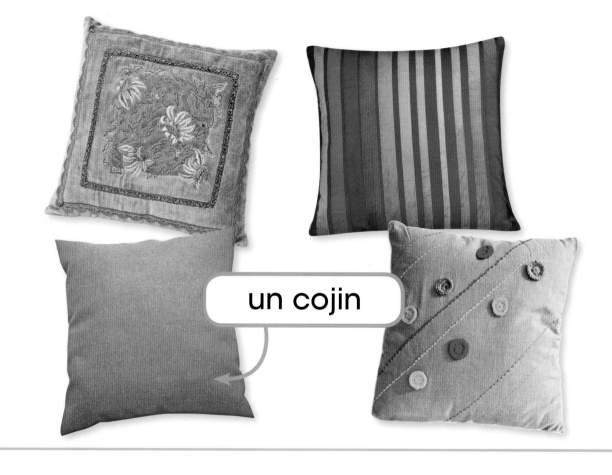

un cojin

Hay cuatro cojines.

There are four cushions.

Cinco

un juguete

Hay cinco juguetes.

There are five toys.

un libro

Hay cinco libros.

There are five books.

Seis

un abrigo

Hay seis abrigos.

There are six coats.

un lápiz

Hay seis lápices.

There are six pencils.

Siete

una naranja

Hay siete naranjas.

There are seven oranges.

una galleta

Hay siete galletas.

There are seven biscuits.

Ocho

un coche

Hay ocho coches.

There are eight cars.

un sombrero

Hay ocho sombreros.

There are eight hats.

Nueve

un globo

Hay nueve globos.

There are nine balloons.

una vela

Hay nueve velas.

There are nine candles.

Diez

una manzana

Hay diez manzanas.

There are ten apples.

una flor

Hay diez flores.

There are ten flowers.

Dictionary

Spanish word	How to say it	English word
abrigo / abrigos	abb-ree-go	coat / coats
chica / chicas	chee-ca / chee-cas	girl / girls
cinco	thin-co	five
coche / coches	cotch-ay / cotch-ays	car / cars
cojin / cojines	co-jin /co-jin-es	cushion / cushions
cuatro	quat-tro	four
diez	dee-eth	ten
dos	doss	two
flor / flores	floor / floo-rays	flower / flowers
galleta / galletas	guy-etta/ guy-ettas	biscuit / biscuits
gato / gatos	ga-to /gat-os	cat / cats
globo / globos	glo-bo / glo-bos	balloon / balloons
hay	I (as in "pie")	there is / there are
juguete / juguetes	who-get-ay / who-get-ays	toy / toys
lápiz / lápices	laa-peeth / laa-pee-thays	pencil / pencils
libro / libros	lee-bro / lee-bros	book / books

Spanish word	How to say it	English word
manzana / manzanas	man-than-na / man-than-nas	apple / apples
naranja / naranjas	na-ran-ha / na-ran-has	orange / oranges
nueve	noo-e-bay	nine
ocho	otch-o	eight
pájaro / pájaros	paa-ha-ro / paa-ha-ros	bird / birds
perro	per-ro	dog
seis	say-ees	six
siete	see-et-tay	seven
silla / sillas	see-ya / see-yas	chair / chairs
sombrero / sombreros	som-brer-ro / som-brer-ros	hat / hats
suéter	sweater	jumper
tres	trayss	three
un / una	oo-n / oo-nah	a
un / una / uno	oo-n / oo-nah / oo-noh	one
vela / velas	bella / bellas	candle / candles
zapato / zapatos	tha-pat-o / tha-pat-os	shoe / shoes

Index

Notes for parents and teachers
In Spanish, nouns are either masculine or feminine. The word for "a" or "one"
changes accordingly – either un (masculine) or una (feminine). "Uno" is used
when you write the number one on its own rather than as part of a sentence.

Quentin Blake

ANGEL PAVEMENT

A Tom Maschler Book
JONATHAN CAPE
LONDON

To all my friends who like drawing

This book about drawing was inspired by two ventures: the Campaign for Drawing and its annual Big Draw, and the proposed Quentin Blake Gallery of Illustration. It is published with greetings to the directors and patrons of the first, and to the trustees and supporters of the second, some of whom appear in disguise in these pages. The book is partly drawn with a multicoloured pencil produced for the British Council exhibition 'Magic Pencil', which I curated with Andrea Rose and which is at present on its world tour.

You can find out about each of these, as well as other books and projects, on **www.quentinblake.com.**

ANGEL PAVEMENT
A JONATHAN CAPE BOOK: 0 224 07027 4

Published in Great Britain by Jonathan Cape,
an imprint of Random House Children's Books

This edition published 2004

1 3 5 7 9 10 8 6 4 2

Copyright © Quentin Blake, 2004

The right of Quentin Blake to be identified as
the author and illustrator of this work has been asserted
in accordance with the Copyright, Designs and Patents Act, 1988

RANDOM HOUSE CHILDREN'S BOOKS
61–63 Uxbridge Road, London W5 5SA
A division of The Random House Group Ltd
RANDOM HOUSE AUSTRALIA (PTY) LTD
20 Alfred Street, Milsons Point, Sydney,
New South Wales 2061, Australia
RANDOM HOUSE NEW ZEALAND LTD
18 Poland Road, Glenfield, Auckland 10, New Zealand
RANDOM HOUSE (PTY) LTD
Endulini, 5A Jubilee Road, Parktown 2193, South Africa

THE RANDOM HOUSE GROUP Limited Reg. No. 954009
www.kidsatrandomhouse.co.uk

A CIP catalogue record for this book is available from the British Library

Printed and bound in Hong Kong

This story is about two girls called Loopy and Corky.
They were unusual, and on the next page you will see why.

They were unusual because they were angels.
Most people didn't know that, because in
real life their wings don't show up. But this
is a picture book, so you can see them.

Loopy and Corky hardly knew they were angels, because in every other way they were just like us.

They liked chocolate biscuits. Loopy could put a whole one in her mouth at once.

They liked fizzy drinks. Corky could drink so much that her eyes whizzed round like Catherine wheels.

Sometimes they would have an argument,
and Corky would scream at Loopy.

And then Loopy would scream back.

And sometimes they would scream together,
just for the sheer pleasure of it.

So you see they were perfectly normal girls.

They also both liked drawing.
   They had all kinds of crayons,
      chalks, pens and markers that they had collected
         from people's dustbins and wastepaper baskets.

They drew on old
wrapping paper, wallpaper,
wastepaper: any kind of paper.
They drew for hours on end.

Loopy was very good at drawing soldiers in uniform and people with toothache.

Corky was very good at drawing dogs and birds with lovely tails.

It was because they liked drawing that they thought they would go and see Sid Bunkin, the pavement artist.

He had just finished a cheerful picture of a laughing cavalier, but he didn't look very happy himself.

'Tomorrow is the Big Drawing
Competition, but there's no way
the judges are going to see my pictures.
It's hopeless for a pavement artist…

'Either people walk over your
pictures on their way home…
or it rains and they're all
washed into the gutter.

'And if you lift up the paving stones
you get into trouble.'

'I know what,' said Corky. 'We can give you a special pencil from our collection. It draws in the air and it's absolutely heavenly.'

'Simply angelic,' said Loopy.

'Totally divine,' said Corky.

'You still have to know how to draw, though.'

Sid Bunkin had a go with Loopy and Corky's pencil.
It really did draw in the air.
    He drew a fish...

...and two birds...

...and an acrobat.

Then Loopy and Corky grabbed him by the braces and off they went, up and up like a helicopter over the town.

They went past the new building site...

...and over the old traffic bridge.

They went past the
Town Clock Tower…

the Griswold
Building…

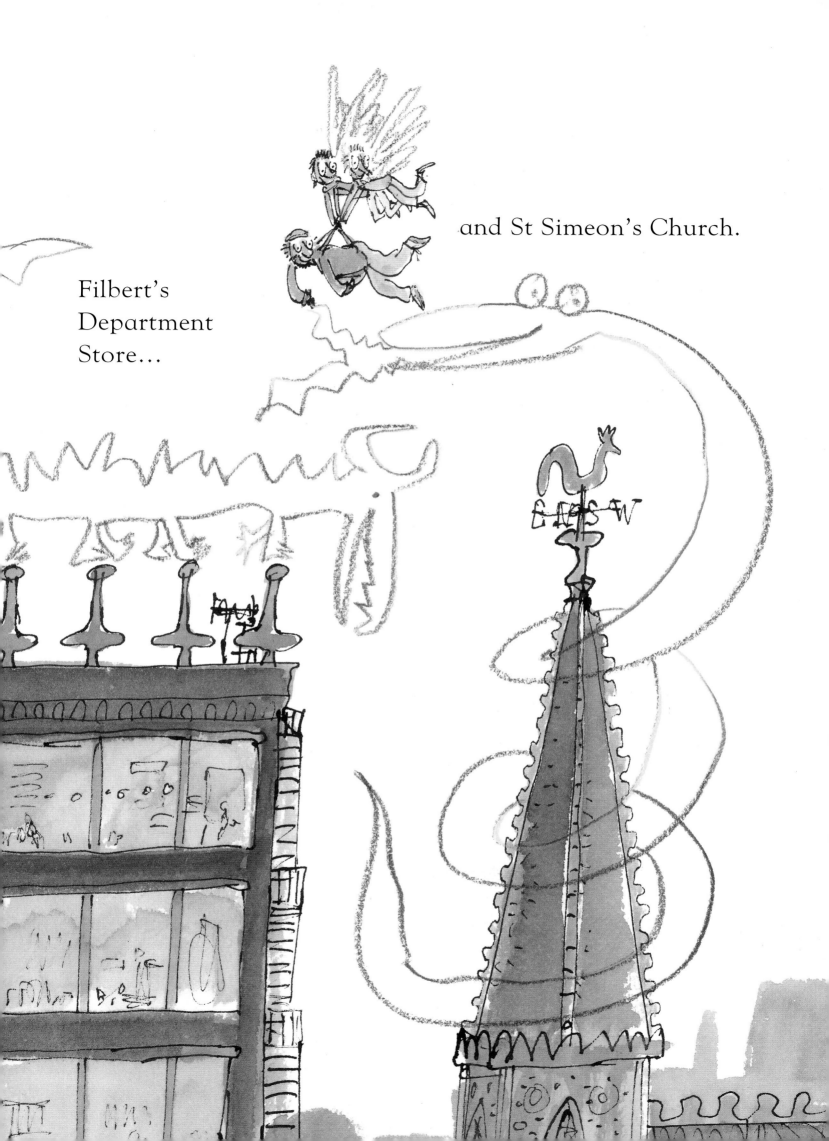

Filbert's
Department
Store...

and St Simeon's Church.

They went over the Brick Street school playground…

...and the Sunset Retirement Home.

The Big Drawing Competition was in Prospect Park.
All their friends were there – George and Jo
and Dave and Gigs, Big Rob and Little Zip
– and lots of other people.

They had never seen drawings in the air before – it was just amazing!

Then the judges gave the prizes.

There were prizes for drawing animals and birds...

...portraits of your family...

...monsters...

...and where you spent your holidays.

Sid Bunkin was awarded the prize for the best surprise drawing.

Everyone clapped and cheered, especially Loopy and Corky and their friends.

Next morning, Sid Bunkin
went back to working on the
pavement with the best quality
Artist's Pastels which were
part of his drawing prize.

But later on in the day,
when there were not many
people about, he took
the special pencil from
behind his left ear.

This time – can you believe it – the drawings took
to the air on their own, even though Sid Bunkin
stayed just where he was.

Up and up they went, all over the town.
It was extraordinary.
  But then, when you start drawing you can
never be quite sure what is going to happen
next, can you?